Vegetarian Barbecues

STEP-BY-STEP

Vegetarian Barbecues

SUE ASHWORTH

SHOOTING STAR PRESS

This edition printed in 1995 for:
Shooting Star Press Inc
230 Fifth Avenue – Suite 1212
New York, NY 10001

Shooting Star Press books are available at special discounts for bulk purchases for sales promotions, premiums, fund-raising, or educational use. Special edition or book excerpts can also be created to specification. For details contact: Special Sales Director, Shooting Star Press Inc., 230 Fifth Avenue, Suite 1212, New York, NY 10001

ISBN 1-57335-004-4

Produced by Haldane Mason, London

Printed in Italy

Acknowledgements:
Art Direction: Ron Samuels
Editor: Joanna Swinnerton
Series Design: Pedro & Frances Prá-Lopez/Kingfisher Design
Page Design: Somewhere Creative
Photography and styling: Iain Bagwell
Home Economist: Sue Ashworth
Assistant Home Economist: Yvonne Melville

Photographs on pages 6, 20, 34, 48 and 62 are reproduced by permission of
ZEFA Picture Library (UK) Ltd.

The photographer would like to thank Ceramica Blue and Webber Barbecues
for the loan of props.

Note:
Unless otherwise stated, milk is assumed to be full-fat, eggs are AA large and pepper is freshly ground black pepper.

Contents

CHAPTER ONE

Dips, Sauces & Marinades

In this chapter, you will find some delicious ideas for tasty dips, a spicy barbecue sauce, rich marinades and lively dressings – those all-important details that complete the barbecue, and make the food taste superb. There are some great barbecue basics here, designed to excite the palate, and to add to the flavor of the finished food.

One point that is crucial to the whole idea of outdoor eating is that although the food should be simple and easy to prepare, it should still taste wonderful. All the ideas in this chapter have been developed with that aim in mind. Here you will find recipes that are quick to put together, taking only moments to assemble.

When marinating food, it is a good idea to prepare it several hours before the barbecue, so that it has plenty of time to soak up the flavors of the marinade. The same principle applies to the sauces, dips and dressings too, as the longer the ingredients are combined, the more the flavors will develop and mellow. Besides, the earlier these are prepared, the less you will have to do at the barbecue!

Opposite: A simple dressing made with fresh herbs, spices, aromatic oils, sharp vinegars and a range of fruit and vegetable ingredients will add an invaluable flavor to your barbecued food.

STEP 1

STEP 2

STEP 3

STEP 4

BUTTERED NUT & LENTIL DIP

This tasty dip is very easy to make. It is perfect to have at barbecues, as it gives your guests something to nibble while they are waiting for their cooked food.

SERVES 4

¹/₄ cup butter
1 small onion, chopped
¹/₃ cup red lentils
1¹/₄ cups vegetable stock
¹/₂ cup blanched almonds
¹/₂ cup pine nuts
¹/₂ tsp ground coriander
¹/₂ tsp ground cumin
¹/₂ tsp freshly grated gingerroot
1 tsp chopped fresh cilantro
salt and pepper
sprigs of fresh cilantro to garnish

TO SERVE:
fresh vegetable crudités
bread sticks

1 Melt half the butter in a saucepan, and fry the onion slowly until golden-brown.

2 Add the lentils and stock. Bring to a boil, then reduce the heat and simmer, uncovered, for 25–30 minutes until the lentils are tender. Drain well.

3 Melt the remaining butter in a small skillet. Add the almonds and pine nuts and fry them slowly until golden-brown. Remove from the heat.

4 Put the lentils, almonds and pine nuts, with any remaining butter, into a blender or food processor. Add the ground coriander, cumin, ginger and fresh cilantro. Blend until smooth, about 15–20 seconds. Alternatively, push the lentils through a strainer to purée them, and mix with the finely chopped nuts, spices and herbs.

5 Season the dip with salt and pepper, and garnish with sprigs of fresh cilantro. Serve with fresh vegetable crudités and bread sticks.

VARIATIONS

Green or brown lentils can be used, but they will take longer to cook than red lentils.

If you wish, substitute peanuts for the almonds to make a more economical version.

Ground ginger can be used instead of fresh gingerroot – substitute ¹/₄ teaspoon and add it to the food processor or blender with the other spices.

STEP 1

STEP 2

STEP 3

STEP 4

TZATZIKI WITH POCKET BREADS & BLACK OLIVE DIP

Tzatziki is a Greek dish, made with natural yogurt, mint and cucumber. It tastes superb with warm pocket bread and the black olive dip provides a delicious contrast of flavor.

SERVES 4

$^1/_2$ English cucumber
1 cup thick natural yogurt
1 tbsp chopped fresh mint
salt and pepper
4 pocket breads

DIP:
2 garlic cloves, crushed
$^3/_4$ cup pitted black olives
4 tbsp olive oil
2 tbsp lemon juice
1 tbsp chopped fresh parsley

TO GARNISH:
sprigs of fresh mint
sprigs of fresh parsley

1 To make the tzatziki, peel the cucumber, and chop roughly. Sprinkle it with salt, and let rest for 15–20 minutes. Rinse with cold water, and drain well.

2 Mix the cucumber, yogurt and mint together. Season with salt and pepper, and transfer to a serving bowl. Cover and chill for 20–30 minutes.

3 To make the dip, put the crushed garlic and olives into a blender or food processor, and blend for 15–20 seconds. Alternatively, chop them very finely.

4 Add the olive oil, lemon juice and parsley to the blender or food processor, and blend for a few more seconds. Alternatively, mix with the chopped garlic and olives and mash together. Season with salt and pepper.

5 Wrap the pocket breads in foil, and place over the barbecue for 2–3 minutes, turning once to warm through. Alternatively, heat in the oven, or under the broiler. Cut into pieces, and serve with the tzatziki and black olive dip, garnished with sprigs of fresh mint and parsley.

TIPS

Sprinkling the cucumber with salt draws out some of its moisture, making it crisper. If you are in a hurry, you can omit this procedure.
  Use green olives instead of black ones if you prefer.

HEAVENLY GARLIC DIP WITH CRUDITÉS

Anyone who loves garlic will adore this dip – it is very potent! Keep it warm over the hot coals to one side of the barbecue, and dip raw vegetables or hunks of French bread into it.

STEP 1

ERVES 4

bulbs garlic
tbsp olive oil
small onion, finely chopped
tbsp lemon juice
tbsp tahini (sesame seed paste)
tbsp chopped fresh parsley
alt and pepper

O SERVE:
resh vegetable crudités
rench bread or warmed pocket breads

1 Separate the bulbs of garlic into individual cloves. Place them on a aking sheet, and roast in a preheated ven at 400°F for 8–10 minutes. Let cool or a few minutes.

2 Peel the garlic cloves, then chop them finely.

3 Heat the olive oil in a saucepan or skillet, and add the chopped garlic nd chopped onion. Fry slowly for 8–10 minutes until softened. Remove the pan rom the heat.

4 Mix the lemon juice, tahini and parsley into the garlic mixture. eason to taste with salt and pepper.

Transfer to a small heatproof bowl, and keep warm at one side of the barbecue.

5 Serve with fresh vegetable crudités, chunks of French bread or warm pocket breads.

STEP 2

STEP 3

SMOKED GARLIC

If you come across smoked garlic, use it in this recipe – it tastes wonderful. There is no need to roast the smoked garlic, so omit the first step.

This dip can also be used to baste kebabs and vegetarian burgers.

STEP 4

13

STEP 1

STEP 2

STEP 3

STEP 4

TASTY BARBECUE SAUCE

Just the thing for brushing onto vegetable kebabs and burgers, this sauce takes only minutes to make.

SERVES 4

2 tbsp butter or margarine
1 garlic clove, crushed
1 onion, finely chopped
1 3-ounce can of chopped tomatoes
1 tbsp dark muscovado sugar
1 tsp hot chili sauce
1–2 gherkins
1 tbsp capers, drained
salt and pepper

1 Melt the butter or margarine in a saucepan, and fry the garlic and onion until well browned, about 8–10 minutes.

2 Add the chopped tomatoes, sugar and chili sauce. Bring to a boil, then reduce the heat and simmer slowly for 20–25 minutes, until thick and pulpy.

3 Chop the gherkins and capers finely.

4 Add the chopped gherkins and capers to the sauce, stirring well to mix. Cook the sauce for an additional 2 minutes.

5 Taste the sauce, and season with a little salt and pepper. Use as a baste for vegetarian kebabs and burgers, or as an accompaniment to other barbecued food.

TIPS

To make sure that the sauce has a good color, it is important to brown the onions really well to begin with.

When fresh tomatoes are cheap and plentiful, they can be used instead of canned ones. Peel and chop 1 pound, and add them as before.

Substitute chili powder instead of chili sauce, according to taste. If you prefer a milder version of barbecue sauce, leave it out altogether.

STEP 1

STEP 2

STEP 3

STEP 4

CITRUS & FRESH HERB MARINADE

Choose one of these marinades to give a marvelous flavor to the food that is to be barbecued. Or just use them for brushing onto the food while it cooks over the hot coals.

EACH DRESSING SERVES 4

ORANGE, CHIVE & MARJORAM:
1 orange
1/2 cup olive oil
4 tbsp dry white wine
4 tbsp white wine vinegar
1 tbsp snipped fresh chives
1 tbsp chopped fresh marjoram
salt and pepper

THAI-SPICED LIME & CILANTRO:
1 stalk lemon grass
finely grated rind and juice of 1 lemon
4 tbsp sesame oil
2 tbsp light soy sauce
pinch of ground ginger
1 tbsp chopped fresh cilantro
salt and pepper

BASIL, LEMON & OREGANO:
finely grated rind of 1 lemon
4 tbsp lemon juice
1 tbsp balsamic vinegar
2 tbsp red wine vinegar
2 tbsp virgin olive oil
1 tbsp chopped fresh oregano
1 tbsp chopped fresh basil
salt and pepper

1 To make the Orange, Chive & Marjoram Marinade, remove the rind from the orange with a zester, or grate it finely, then squeeze the juice.

2 Mix the orange rind and juice with all the remaining ingredients in a small bowl, whisking together to combine. Season with salt and pepper.

3 To make the Thai-spiced Lime & Cilantro Marinade, bruise the lemon grass by crushing it with a rolling pin. Mix the remaining ingredients together, and add the lemon grass.

4 To make the Basil, Lemon & Oregano Marinade, whisk all the ingredients together in a small bowl. Season with salt and pepper.

5 Keep the marinades covered with plastic wrap or store in screw-top jars, ready for using as marinades or bastes.

STEP 1

STEP 2

STEP 3

STEP 4

TRIO OF FAVORITE DRESSINGS

You can rely on any one of these delicious dressings to bring out the very best in your salads.

EACH DRESSING SERVES 4

*WHOLE GRAIN MUSTARD & CIDER
    VINEGAR DRESSING:*
^{1}/$_2$ cup olive oil
4 tbsp cider vinegar
2 tsp whole grain mustard
^{1}/$_2$ tsp superfine sugar
salt and pepper

GARLIC & PARSLEY DRESSING:
1 small garlic clove
1 tbsp fresh parsley
^{2}/$_3$ cup light cream
4 tbsp natural yogurt
1 tsp lemon juice
pinch of superfine sugar
salt and pepper

*RASPBERRY & HAZELNUT
    VINAIGRETTE:*
4 tbsp raspberry vinegar
4 tbsp light olive oil
4 tbsp hazelnut oil
^{1}/$_2$ tsp superfine sugar
2 tsp chopped fresh chives
salt and pepper

1 To make the Whole Grain Mustard & Cider Vinegar Dressing, whisk all the ingredients together in a small bowl.

2 To make the Garlic & Parsley Dressing, crush the garlic clove, and chop the parsley finely.

3 Mix the garlic and parsley with the remaining ingredients. Whisk together until combined. Cover and chill for 30 minutes.

4 To make the Raspberry & Hazelnut Vinaigrette, whisk all the ingredients together until combined.

5 Keep the dressings covered with plastic wrap or sealed in screw-top jars. Chill until ready for use.

SERVING SUGGESTIONS

Whole Grain Mustard & Cider Vinegar Dressing is excellent with a tomato salad. Garlic & Parsley Dressing tastes delicious as a coating for potato salad, and Raspberry & Hazelnut Vinaigrette makes a superb dressing for mixed salad greens.

CHAPTER TWO

Filled Things

Easy-to-eat food is essential for barbecues. More often than not, barbecued food is eaten while standing up and moving around, and it is tricky trying to balance a plate, eat from it, hold a glass and have a conversation at the same time! Hopefully, the ideas in this section will help to make the balancing act a little easier.

By providing a range of filled foods such as pocket and naan breads, baguettes, baked potatoes, burger rolls and the occasional stuffed vegetable, you will be offering self-contained food that is easy to eat and enjoy – a movable feast! What's more, these ideas are perfect for children, who never seem to sit still for a moment.

The choices offered in this section are deliciously different and very tasty. Try, for instance, the Naan Bread with Curried Vegetable Kebabs – a mouthwatering recipe for barbecued kebabs brushed with a spicy combination of coriander, cumin and chili powder blended in natural yogurt. Served with Indian bread warmed over the hot coals, it really is a winner.

Opposite: The setting sun provides a perfect backdrop for an unforgettable barbecue.

21

STEP 1

STEP 2

STEP 3

STEP 4

FILLED BAKED POTATOES

Cook these potatoes conventionally, then wrap them in foil, and keep them warm at the edge of the barbecue, ready to fill with a choice of three inspired mixtures.

EACH DRESSING SERVES 4

4 large or 8 medium baking potatoes

MEXICAN CORN RELISH:
8-ounce can of corn, drained
$^1/_2$ red bell pepper, cored, deseeded, and finely
    chopped
2-in. piece English cucumber, finely chopped
$^1/_2$ tsp chili powder
salt and pepper

BLUE CHEESE, CELERY & CHIVE
    FILLING:
$^1/_2$ cup cream cheese
$^1/_2$ cup natural fromage frais
4 ounces blue cheese, cut into cubes
1 celery stalk, finely chopped
2 tsp snipped fresh chives
celery salt and pepper

MUSHROOMS IN SPICY TOMATO
    SAUCE:
2 tbsp butter or margarine
3 cups button mushrooms
$^2/_3$ cup natural yogurt
1 tbsp tomato paste
2 tsp mild curry powder
salt and pepper
paprika or chili powder, or chopped fresh
    herbs, to garnish

1 Scrub the potatoes and prick them with a fork. Bake in a preheated oven at 400°F for about 1 hour, until just tender.

2 To make the Mexican Corn Relish, put half the corn into a bowl. Put the remainder into a blender or food processor for 10–15 seconds, or chop and mash roughly by hand. Add the puréed corn to the corn kernels with the bell pepper, cucumber and chili powder. Season to taste.

3 To make the Blue Cheese, Celery & Chive Filling, mix the cream cheese and fromage frais together until smooth. Add the blue cheese, celery, and chives. Season with pepper and celery salt.

4 To make the Mushrooms in Spicy Tomato Sauce, melt the butter or margarine in a small skillet. Add the mushrooms, and cook slowly for 3–4 minutes. Remove from the heat, and stir in the yogurt, tomato paste, and curry powder. Season to taste.

5 Wrap the cooked potatoes in foil, and keep warm at the edge of the barbecue. Serve the fillings sprinkled with paprika or chili powder, or herbs.

STEP 1

STEP 2

STEP 3

STEP 4

MELTING CHEESE & ONION BAGUETTES

Part-baked baguettes are split and filled with a tasty cheese and onion mixture, then wrapped in foil and cooked over the barbecue to make them warm, crisp and delicious.

SERVES 4

4 part-baked baguettes
2 tbsp tomato relish
1/4 cup butter
8 scallions, trimmed and finely chopped
1/2 cup cream cheese
1 cup grated Cheddar cheese
1 tsp snipped fresh chives
pepper

TO SERVE:
mixed salad greens
fresh herbs

1 Split the part-baked baguettes in half lengthways, without cutting right through. Spread a little tomato relish on each split baguette.

2 Melt the butter in a skillet and add the scallions. Fry them slowly until softened and golden. Remove from the heat, and let cool slightly.

3 Beat the cream cheese in a mixing bowl to soften it. Mix in the scallions, with any remaining butter. Add the grated cheese and snipped chives, and mix well. Season with a little pepper.

4 Divide the cheese mixture between the baguettes. Spread it over the cut surfaces, and sandwich the halves together. Wrap each baguette tightly in foil.

5 Heat the baguettes over the barbecue for about 10–15 minutes, turning them occasionally. Peel back the foil to check that they are cooked, and the cheese mixture has melted. Serve garnished with mixed salad greens and fresh herbs.

TIME SAVER

If there's no room on the barbecue, and you want to eat these at the same time as the rest of the food, bake them in a preheated oven at 400°F for 15 minutes.

CHEESEBURGERS IN ROLLS WITH BARBECUE SAUCE

Soy mince and seasonings combine to make these tasty vegetarian burgers, which are topped with cheese, barbecue sauce, dill pickle, cucumber, and tomato.

STEP 1

SERVES 4

¹/₃ cup dehydrated soy granules (TVP)
2¹/₄ cups vegetable stock
1 small onion, finely chopped
1 cup all-purpose flour
1 egg, beaten
1 tbsp chopped fresh herbs
1 tbsp mushroom ketchup or soy sauce
2 tbsp vegetable oil
4 burger rolls
4 cheese slices
salt and pepper

TO GARNISH:
Tasty Barbecue Sauce (see page 14)
dill pickles
tomato slices

TO SERVE:
lettuce
English cucumber
scallions

1 Put the dehydrated soy granules into a large bowl. Pour over the vegetable stock, and let the granules soak for about 15 minutes until it has been absorbed.

2 Add the onion, flour, beaten egg, and chopped herbs. Season with the mushroom ketchup or soy sauce and a little salt and pepper.

3 Form the mixture into 8 burgers. Cover and chill until ready to cook.

4 Brush the burgers with vegetable oil, and barbecue them over hot coals, turning once. Allow about 5 minutes on each side.

5 Split the rolls and top with a burger. Lay a cheese slice on top, and garnish with barbecue sauce, dill pickle, and tomato slices. Serve with a green salad made with the lettuce, English cucumber, and scallions.

STEP 2

STEP 3

VARIATIONS

Flavor the burgers with different fresh herbs to vary the taste, or use mixed dried herbs for convenience.

Give the burgers a spicy flavor by adding ¹/₂–1 teaspoon of chili powder to the mixture.

STEP 5

27

STEP 1

STEP 2

STEP 3

STEP 4

NAAN BREAD WITH CURRIED VEGETABLE KEBABS

Warmed Indian bread is served with barbecued vegetable kebabs, which are brushed with a curry-spiced yogurt baste.

SERVES 4

4 metal or wooden skewers (soak wooden skewers in warm water for 30 minutes)

YOGURT BASTE:
²/₃ cup natural yogurt
1 tbsp chopped fresh mint (or 1 tsp dried)
1 tsp ground cumin
1 tsp ground coriander
¹/₂ tsp chili powder
pinch of turmeric
pinch of ground ginger
salt and pepper

KEBABS:
8 small new potatoes
1 small eggplant
1 zucchini, cut into chunks
8 crimini or closed-cup mushrooms
8 small tomatoes
naan bread to serve
sprigs of fresh mint to garnish

1 To make the spiced yogurt baste, mix together the yogurt, mint, cumin, coriander, chili powder, turmeric and ginger. Season with salt and pepper. Cover and chill.

2 Boil the potatoes until just tender. Meanwhile, chop the eggplant into chunks, and sprinkle them liberally with salt. Let rest for 10–15 minutes to extract the bitter juices. Rinse and drain them well. Drain the potatoes.

3 Thread the vegetables onto the skewers, alternating the different types.

4 Place them in a shallow dish, and brush with the yogurt baste, coating them evenly. Cover and chill until ready to cook.

5 Wrap the naan bread in foil, and place toward one side of the barbecue to warm through.

6 Cook the kebabs over the barbecue, basting with any remaining spiced yogurt, until they just begin to char slightly. Serve with the warmed Indian bread, garnished with sprigs of fresh mint.

VARIATION

Try using these curried vegetables to fill warmed and split pocket breads. Serve with a refreshing salad of shredded lettuce, English cucumber and tomatoes.

STEP 1

STEP 2

STEP 3

STEP 4

MEDITERRANEAN STUFFED BELL PEPPERS

Halved bell peppers are stuffed with the flavors of the Mediterranean in this sunshine-bright dish.

SERVES 4

1 red bell pepper
1 green bell pepper
1 yellow bell pepper
1 orange bell pepper
6 tbsp olive oil
1 small red onion, sliced
1 small eggplant, roughly chopped
1½ cups button mushrooms, wiped
1 cup cherry tomatoes, halved
few drops of mushroom ketchup
handful of fresh basil leaves, torn into pieces
2 tbsp lemon juice
salt and pepper
sprigs of fresh basil to garnish
lemon wedges to serve

1 Halve the bell peppers, and remove the cores and seeds. Sprinkle over a few drops of olive oil, and season with a little salt and pepper.

2 Heat the remaining olive oil in a skillet. Add the onion, eggplant, and mushrooms, and fry for 3–4 minutes, stirring frequently. Remove from the heat and transfer to a mixing bowl.

3 Add the cherry tomatoes, mushroom ketchup, basil leaves, and lemon juice to the eggplant mixture. Season well with salt and pepper.

4 Spoon the eggplant mixture into the bell pepper halves. Enclose in foil packages, and cook over the hot coals for about 15–20 minutes, turning once.

5 Unwrap carefully, and serve garnished with sprigs of fresh basil. Serve with lemon wedges.

TIPS

These stuffed bell peppers can be made ahead, and kept in the refrigerator, wrapped in foil, ready for cooking over the barbecue.

Dried herbs can be used if fresh ones are unavailable. Substitute 1 teaspoon of dried basil, or use mixed dried Italian herbs as an alternative.

If you wish, top these stuffed bell peppers with grated Mozzarella or Cheddar cheese – ¼ cup will be sufficient.

STEP 1

STEP 2

STEP 3

STEP 4

POCKET BREADS WITH GREEK SALAD & HOT ROSEMARY DRESSING

Pocket breads are warmed over the hot coals, then split and filled with a Greek salad tossed in a fragrant rosemary dressing.

SERVES 4

½ iceberg lettuce, roughly chopped
2 large tomatoes, cut into wedges
3-in. piece of English cucumber, cut into
*   chunks*
¼ cup pitted black olives
4 ounces Feta cheese
4 pocket breads

DRESSING:
6 tbsp olive oil
3 tbsp red wine vinegar
1 tbsp crushed fresh rosemary
½ tsp superfine sugar
salt and pepper

1 To make the salad, combine the lettuce, tomatoes, English cucumber and olives.

2 Cut the Feta cheese into chunks, and add to the salad, tossing lightly to combine.

3 To make the dressing, whisk together the oil, vinegar, rosemary and sugar. Season to taste with salt and pepper. Place in a small saucepan or heatproof bowl, and heat slowly, or place over the barbecue to warm through.

4 Wrap the pocket breads tightly in foil, and place over the hot barbecue for 2–3 minutes, turning once, to warm through.

5 Unwrap the breads, and split them open. Fill with the salad mixture, and drizzle over the warm dressing. Serve at once.

ALTERNATIVES

Substitute different herbs for the rosemary – either oregano or basil make delicious alternatives.

Pack plenty of the salad into the pocket breads – they taste much better when packed full to bursting!

CHAPTER THREE

Main Courses

If you thought that vegetarian barbecues consisted of char-grilled mushroom kebabs, then these recipes will make you think again. True, mushrooms do make an appearance in a tempting recipe for brochettes, combined with smoked tofu and basted with olive oil, lemon juice and garlic to make them taste really special. But how about Grilled Cypriot Cheese with Tomato & Red Onion Salad, Barbecued Bean Pot, or Grape Leaf Packages with Soft Cheese & Almonds? Throughout this chapter you will find appealing and imaginative recipes that will really spice up your barbecue!

Some preparation is needed before the barbecue starts, so that certain foods are soaking up their marinades, or are threaded onto skewers in readiness for cooking. The Barbecued Bean Pot needs to be precooked in a conventional oven; the pot is then kept hot over the coals, ready for serving cowboy-style to your hungry guests.

All these recipes provide their fair share of protein – either from cheese, beans, garbanzo beans or tofu. And because they all contain vegetables of some description, they supply important vitamins, minerals and carbohydrates to the diet. Which all adds up to a bonus for food that tastes good too!

Opposite: Use as wide a range of fresh vegetables as you can to create exotic and unusual dishes for your guests.

STEP 1

STEP 2

STEP 3

STEP 4

MOZZARELLA WITH BARBECUED RADICCIO

Sliced Mozzarella cheese is served with sliced tomatoes and radiccio, which is singed over hot coals and drizzled with a basil, olive oil and pesto dressing.

SERVES 4

1 tbsp red or green pesto sauce
6 tbsp virgin olive oil
3 tbsp red wine vinegar
handful of fresh basil leaves
1 pound Mozzarella cheese
4 large tomatoes, sliced
2 radiccio
salt and pepper
fresh basil leaves to garnish

1 To make the dressing, mix the pesto sauce, olive oil and red wine vinegar together.

2 Tear the fresh basil leaves into tiny pieces, and add them to the dressing. Season with a little salt and pepper.

3 Slice the Mozzarella cheese thinly, and arrange it on 4 serving plates with the tomatoes.

4 Leaving the root end on the radiccio, slice each one into quarters. Barbecue them quickly, so that the leaves singe on the outside. Place two quarters on each serving plate.

5 Drizzle the dressing over the radiccio, cheese and tomatoes.

6 Garnish with extra basil leaves and serve immediately.

TIPS

When singeing the radiccio, it is a good idea to barbecue each quarter individually, holding it over the hot coals with tongs and turning it constantly.

If you can't find fresh basil, substitute oregano or marjoram instead. Tearing the basil leaves instead of chopping them helps to retain their peppery fragrance and flavor.

Pesto sauce is an olive oil, basil and pine nut paste that can be bought in jars from supermarkets or delis.

STEP 2

STEP 3

STEP 4

STEP 5

SMOKED TOFU & MUSHROOM BROCHETTES

These tofu and mushroom kebabs are marinated in a lemon, garlic, and herb mixture so that they soak up a delicious flavor.

SERVES 4

8 wooden skewers
1 lemon
1 garlic clove, crushed
4 tbsp olive oil
4 tbsp white wine vinegar
1 tbsp chopped fresh herbs, such as
    rosemary, parsley, and thyme
10 ounces smoked tofu
1 1/2 cups mushrooms, wiped
salt and pepper
fresh herbs to garnish

TO SERVE:
mixed salad greens
cherry tomatoes, halved

1 Soak the wooden skewers in hand-hot water for 30 minutes.

2 Grate the rind from the lemon finely, and squeeze out the juice.

3 Add the garlic, olive oil, vinegar, and herbs to the lemon rind and juice, mixing well. Season with salt and pepper.

4 Slice the tofu into large chunks. Thread the pieces onto the skewers, alternating them with the mushrooms.

5 Lay the kebabs in a shallow dish, and pour over the marinade. Cover and chill for 1–2 hours, turning the kebabs in the marinade occasionally.

6 Cook the kebabs over the barbecue, brushing them with the marinade and turning often, for about 6 minutes.

7 Garnish with fresh herbs and serve with mixed salad greens and cherry tomatoes.

EXTRA FLAVOR

Firm tofu can be substituted for the smoked variety if you prefer.

Thread small fresh bay leaves onto the skewers. They will help to give the kebabs a good flavor.

STEP 1

STEP 2

STEP 3

STEP 5

GRAPE-LEAF PACKAGES WITH SOFT CHEESE & ALMONDS

A wonderful combination of cream cheese, chopped dates, ground almonds and lightly fried nuts is encased in grape leaves, which are wrapped in foil and cooked over the barbecue.

SERVES 4

1¼ cups cream cheese
¼ cup ground almonds
2 tbsp dates, pitted and chopped
2 tbsp butter
¼ cup slivered almonds
12–16 grape leaves
salt and pepper

TO GARNISH:
sprigs of rosemary
tomato wedges

1 Beat the cream cheese in a large bowl to soften it.

2 Add the ground almonds and chopped dates, and mix together thoroughly. Season with salt and pepper.

3 Melt the butter in a small skillet. Add the slivered almonds, and fry them slowly for 2–3 minutes until golden brown. Remove from the heat, and let cool for a few minutes.

4 Mix the fried nuts with the cream cheese mixture, stirring well to combine thoroughly.

5 Soak the grape leaves in water to remove some of the saltiness, if specified on the package. Drain them, lay them out on a counter and spoon an equal amount of the cream cheese mixture onto each one. Fold over the leaves to enclose the filling.

6 Wrap the grape leaf packages in foil, 1 or 2 per foil package. Place over the barbecue to heat through for about 8–10 minutes, turning once.

7 Serve with barbecued baby corn, and garnish with sprigs of rosemary and tomato wedges.

VARIATION

Omit the dates from the filling, and substitute golden raisins or raisins. Ground and whole hazelnuts can be used instead of almonds.

TURKISH VEGETABLE KEBABS WITH SPICY GARBANZO BEAN SAUCE

A spicy garbanzo bean sauce is served with barbecued vegetable kebabs.

SERVES 4

4 metal or wooden skewers (soak wooden
    skewers in warm water for 30 minutes)

SAUCE:
4 tbsp olive oil
3 garlic cloves, crushed
1 small onion, finely chopped
1 5-ounce can of garbanzo beans, rinsed and
    drained
1¼ cups natural yogurt
1 tsp cumin
½ tsp chili powder
lemon juice
salt and pepper

KEBABS:
1 eggplant
1 red bell pepper, cored and deseeded
1 green bell pepper, cored and deseeded
4 plum tomatoes
1 lemon, cut into wedges
8 small fresh bay leaves
olive oil for brushing

1 To make the sauce, heat the olive oil in a small skillet and fry the garlic and onion slowly until softened and golden brown, about 5 minutes.

STEP 1

2 Put the garbanzo beans and yogurt into a blender or food processor, and add the cumin, chili powder and onion mixture. Blend for about 15 seconds until smooth. Alternatively, mash the garbanzo beans and mix with the yogurt, cumin, chili powder and softened onion.

STEP 2

3 Tip the puréed mixture into a bowl, and season to taste with lemon juice, salt and pepper. Cover and chill until ready to serve.

4 To prepare the kebabs, cut the vegetables into large chunks, and thread them onto the skewers, placing a bay leaf and lemon wedge at both ends of each kebab.

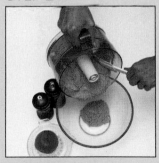

STEP 3

5 Brush the kebabs with olive oil, and cook them over the barbecue, turning frequently, for about 5–8 minutes. Heat the garbanzo bean sauce, and serve with the kebabs.

MILDER SAUCE

To make a sauce with a milder flavor, substitute paprika for the chili powder.

STEP 4

43

STEP 1

STEP 2

STEP 3

STEP 4

BARBECUED BEAN POT

Cook this tasty vegetable and TVP casserole conventionally, then keep it piping hot over the barbecue. Its delicious aroma will cut through the fresh air to make appetites very keen!

SERVES 4

¼ cup butter or margarine
1 large onion, chopped
2 garlic cloves, crushed
2 carrots, sliced
2 celery stalks, sliced
1 tbsp paprika
2 tsp ground cumin
14-ounce can of chopped tomatoes
15-ounce can of mixed beans, rinsed and
   drained
⅔ cup vegetable stock
1 tbsp molasses sugar or molasses
12 ounces TVP (soy) cubes
salt and pepper

1 Melt the butter or margarine in a large flameproof casserole, and fry the onion and garlic slowly for about 5 minutes, until golden brown.

2 Add the carrots and celery, and cook for an additional 2 minutes, then stir in the paprika and cumin.

3 Add the tomatoes and mixed beans. Pour in the vegetable stock, and add the molasses sugar or molasses. Bring to a boil, then reduce the heat and simmer, uncovered, for 30 minutes, stirring occasionally.

4 Add the TVP cubes to the casserole and cook, covered, for an additional 20 minutes. Stir the mixture occasionally.

5 Season to taste, then transfer the casserole to the barbecue, keeping it to one side to keep hot.

6 Ladle onto plates, and serve with crusty French bread.

ALTERNATIVES

If you prefer, cook the casserole in a preheated oven at 375°F from step 3, but keep the dish covered.
   Instead of mixed beans you could use just one type of canned beans. Choose from red kidney beans, black-eyed peas, garbanzo beans or soya beans.

STEP 2

STEP 3

STEP 4

STEP 6

GRILLED CYPRIOT CHEESE WITH TOMATO & RED ONION SALAD

Haloumi is a type of Cypriot cheese which remains firm and takes on a marvelous flavor when swiftly barbecued.

SERVES 4

1 pound Haloumi cheese
½ quantity Orange, Chive & Marjoram
  Marinade (see page 16)

SALAD:
8 ounces plum tomatoes
1 small red onion
4 tbsp olive oil
2 tbsp cider vinegar
1 tsp lemon juice
pinch of ground coriander
2 tsp chopped fresh cilantro
salt and pepper
fresh basil leaves to garnish

1 Slice the cheese quite thickly, and place it in a shallow dish.

2 Pour the marinade over the cheese. Cover and chill for at least 30 minutes.

3 To make the salad, slice the tomatoes, and arrange them on a serving plate. Slice the onion thinly, and scatter over the tomatoes.

4 Whisk together the olive oil, vinegar, lemon juice, ground coriander and fresh cilantro.

5 Season to taste with salt and pepper, then drizzle the dressing over the tomatoes and onions. Cover and chill.

6 Drain the marinade from the Haloumi cheese. Cook the cheese over hot coals for 2 minutes, turning once. Lift onto plates, and serve with the salad.

SERVING SUGGESTION

Warmed pocket breads taste wonderful stuffed with the salad, and topped with the barbecued Haloumi.

If Haloumi cheese is not available, you can use Feta cheese instead.

Serve the cheese and salad with crusty bread or potato salad to make it more filling.

CHAPTER FOUR

Salads

Lively salads are an essential accompaniment to barbecued food, supplying a pleasant change of taste and texture to refresh the palate. For something easy and quick to make, you could simply prepare a huge bowl of mixed salad greens, drizzled with one of the dressings from Chapter One, but here you will discover some new ideas for more unusual combinations.

These days it is so easy to make exciting salads with interesting ingredients. All year round, supermarkets and shops are full of glorious vegetables and fruits from all over the world. We can make the most of seasonal, home-grown produce for flavor and economy, or we can buy imported foods for special occasions, or to perk up everyday ingredients to transform them into something special. We can certainly enjoy eating salads throughout the year, even if we can't always rely on the weather for a barbecue!

Any salad is only as good as the ingredients that you put into it, so be sure to choose produce from a reputable supplier, and use it when it is at its best. That way you will be making the most of its freshness and flavor, and you will be getting all the goodness that the fruit and vegetables contain.

Opposite: *Fresh fruits and vegetables used in a range of imaginative salads will provide a refreshing accompaniment to the main course dishes.*

STEP 1

STEP 2

STEP 3

STEP 4

CHAR-GRILLED VEGETABLES WITH SIDEKICK DRESSING

Colorful vegetables are barbecued over hot coals to make this unusual hot salad, which is served with a spicy chili sauce on the side.

SERVES 4

1 red bell pepper, cored and deseeded
1 orange or yellow bell pepper, cored and deseeded
2 zucchini
2 corn-on-the-cob
1 eggplant
olive oil for brushing
chopped fresh thyme, rosemary and parsley
salt and pepper
lime or lemon wedges to serve

DRESSING:
2 tbsp olive oil
1 tbsp sesame oil
1 garlic clove, crushed
1 small onion, finely chopped
1 celery stalk, finely chopped
1 small green chili, deseeded and finely chopped
4 tomatoes, chopped
2-in. piece English cucumber, finely chopped
1 tbsp tomato paste
1 tbsp lime or lemon juice

1 To make the dressing, heat the oils together in a saucepan or skillet. Add the garlic and onion, and fry together slowly until softened, about 3 minutes.

2 Add the celery, chili and tomatoes to the pan, and cook, stirring occasionally, for 5 minutes over a medium heat.

3 Stir in the cucumber, tomato paste and lime or lemon juice, and simmer for 8–10 minutes until thick and pulpy. Season to taste with salt and pepper.

4 Cut the vegetables into thick slices, and brush with a little olive oil.

5 Cook the vegetables over the hot coals for about 5-8 minutes, sprinkling them with salt and pepper and fresh herbs as they cook, and turning once.

6 Divide the vegetables between 4 serving plates, and spoon some of the dressing onto the side. Serve at once, sprinkled with a few more chopped herbs and accompanied by the lime or lemon wedges.

STEP 1

STEP 2

STEP 3

STEP 4

GOAT CHEESE WITH WALNUTS IN WARM OIL & VINEGAR DRESSING

This delicious salad combines soft goat cheese with walnut halves. Served on a bed of mixed salad greens and sprinkled with a warm walnut oil and wine vinegar dressing, it could double as an appetizer.

SERVES 4

1 cup walnut halves
mixed salad greens
4 ounces soft goat cheese
snipped fresh chives to garnish

DRESSING:
6 tbsp walnut oil
3 tbsp white wine vinegar
1 tbsp clear honey
1 tsp Dijon mustard
pinch of ground ginger
salt and pepper

1 To make the dressing, whisk together the walnut oil, wine vinegar, honey, mustard and ginger in a small saucepan. Season to taste.

2 Heat the dressing on the stove top or over the barbecue, stirring occasionally, until warm. Add the walnut halves to the warm dressing, and continue to heat for 3–4 minutes.

3 Arrange the salad leaves on 4 serving plates, and place spoonfuls of goat cheese on top. Lift the walnut halves from the dressing with a perforated spoon, and scatter them over the salads.

4 Transfer the warm dressing to a small jug, for sprinkling over the salads.

5 Sprinkle chives over the salad and serve them, accompanied by the warm walnut oil dressing.

TIPS

Hazelnut oil makes a delicious alternative to walnut oil; if you use it, you can also replace the walnuts with hazelnuts if you wish.

If you are heating the dressing over the barbecue, choose an old saucepan, as it may become blackened on the outside.

CARROT & CASHEW NUT COLESLAW

This simple salad has a brilliant dressing made from poppy seeds pan-fried in sesame oil to bring out their flavor.

STEP 1

SERVES 4

1 large carrot, grated
1 small onion, finely chopped
2 celery stalks, chopped
¼ small, hard white cabbage, shredded
1 tbsp chopped fresh parsley
4 tbsp sesame oil
½ tsp poppy seeds
½ cup cashew nuts
2 tbsp white wine or cider vinegar
salt and pepper
sprigs of fresh parsley to garnish

1 In a large salad bowl, mix together the carrot, onion, celery and cabbage. Stir in the chopped parsley.

2 Heat the sesame oil in a saucepan that has a lid. Add the poppy seeds, and cover the pan. Cook over a medium high heat until the seeds start to make a popping sound. Remove from the heat, and let cool.

3 Scatter the cashew nuts onto a baking sheet. Place them under a medium-hot broiler, and toast until lightly browned, being careful not to burn them. Let cool.

4 Add the vinegar to the oil and poppy seeds, then pour over the carrot mixture. Add the cooled cashew nuts, Toss together to coat the salad ingredients with the dressing.

5 Garnish the salad with sprigs of parsley, and serve.

STEP 2

STEP 3

VARIATIONS

Sesame seeds or sunflower seeds can be used in place of poppy seeds.

Substitute peanuts for cashew nuts if you prefer – they are more economical, and taste every bit as good when lightly toasted.

STEP 4

STEP 1

STEP 2

STEP 3

STEP 4

HONEYDEW & STRAWBERRY SALAD WITH COOL CUCUMBER DRESSING

This refreshing fruit-based salad is perfect for a hot summer's day.

SERVES 4

*¹/₂ iceberg lettuce, shredded
1 small honeydew melon
1¹/₂ cups strawberries, hulled and sliced
2-in. piece of English cucumber, thinly sliced
sprigs of fresh mint to garnish*

*DRESSING:
scant 1 cup natural yogurt
2-in. piece of English cucumber, peeled
a few fresh mint leaves
¹/₂ tsp finely grated lime or lemon rind
pinch of superfine sugar
3–4 ice cubes*

1 Arrange the shredded lettuce on 4 serving plates.

2 Cut the melon lengthways into quarters. Scoop out the seeds, and cut through the flesh down to the skin at 1-in. intervals. Cut the melon close to the skin, and detach the flesh.

3 Place the chunks of melon on the bed of lettuce with the strawberries and cucumber.

4 To make the dressing, put the yogurt, cucumber, mint leaves, lime or lemon rind, superfine sugar, and ice cubes into a blender or food processor. Blend together for about 15 seconds until smooth. Alternatively, chop the cucumber and mint finely, crush the ice cubes, and combine with the other ingredients.

5 Serve the salad with a little dressing poured over it. Garnish with sprigs of fresh mint.

VARIATIONS

Omit the ice cubes in the dressing if you prefer, but make sure that the ingredients are well-chilled. This will insure that the finished dressing is really cool.

Charentais, cantaloupe or ogen melon can be substituted for honeydew.

56

STEP 1

STEP 2

STEP 3

STEP 4

THREE-WAY POTATO SALAD

There's nothing to beat the flavor of new potatoes, served just warm in a delicious dressing.

EACH DRESSING SERVES 4

LIGHT CURRY DRESSING:
1 tbsp vegetable oil
1 tbsp medium curry paste
1 small onion, chopped
1 tbsp mango chutney, chopped
6 tbsp natural yogurt
3 tbsp light cream
2 tbsp mayonnaise
salt and pepper
1 tbsp light cream to garnish

WARM VINAIGRETTE DRESSING:
6 tbsp hazelnut oil
3 tbsp cider vinegar
1 tsp whole grain mustard
1 tsp superfine sugar
few basil leaves, torn into shreds
salt and pepper

PARSLEY, SCALLION & SOUR CREAM
 DRESSING:
²/₃ cup sour cream
3 tbsp light mayonnaise
4 scallions, trimmed and finely chopped
1 tbsp chopped fresh parsley
salt and pepper

1 pound new potatoes for each dressing
fresh herbs to garnish

1 To make the Light Curry Dressing, heat the vegetable oil in a saucepan, and add the curry paste and onion. Fry together, stirring frequently, until the onion is soft, about 5 minutes. Remove from the heat, and let cool slightly.

2 Mix together the mango chutney, yogurt, cream and mayonnaise. Add the curry mixture, and blend together. Season with salt and pepper.

3 To make the Vinaigrette Dressing, whisk the hazelnut oil, cider vinegar, mustard, sugar and basil together in a small jug or bowl. Season with salt and pepper.

4 To make the Parsley, Scallion & Sour Cream Dressing, mix all the ingredients together until thoroughly combined. Season with salt and pepper.

5 Cook the potatoes in lightly salted boiling water until just tender. Drain well, and let cool for 5 minutes, then add the chosen dressing, tossing to coat. Serve, garnished with fresh herbs, spooning a little light cream onto the potatoes if you have used the curry dressing.

STEP 2

STEP 3

STEP 4

STEP 5

DEEP SOUTH SPICED RICE & BEANS

Cajun spices add a flavor of the deep south to this colorful rice and red kidney bean salad.

SERVES 4

scant 1 cup long-grain rice
4 tbsp olive oil
1 small green bell pepper, cored, deseeded
   and chopped
1 small red bell pepper, cored, deseeded and
   chopped
1 onion, finely chopped
1 small red or green chili, deseeded and
   finely chopped
2 tomatoes, chopped
$\frac{1}{2}$ cup canned red kidney beans, rinsed and
   drained
1 tbsp chopped fresh basil
2 tsp chopped fresh thyme (or 1 tsp dried)
1 tsp Cajun spice
salt and pepper
fresh basil leaves to garnish

1 Cook the rice in plenty of boiling, lightly salted water until just tender, about 12 minutes. Rinse with cold water, and drain well.

2 Meanwhile, heat the olive oil in a skillet and fry the green and red bell peppers and onion together slowly until softened, about 5 minutes.

3 Add the chili and tomatoes, and cook for an additional 2 minutes.

4 Add the vegetable mixture and red kidney beans to the rice. Stir well to combine thoroughly.

5 Stir the chopped herbs and Cajun spice into the rice mixture. Season well with salt and pepper, and serve, garnished with basil leaves.

CHILIES

The fresh red or green chili can be replaced by 1 tsp chili powder, for speed and convenience.

   Take care when handling fresh chilies, as the residue from them can burn or irritate the skin. Be especially careful to avoid rubbing your eyes when preparing them, and rinse your hands well after handling them.

CHAPTER FIVE

Desserts

By the time everyone at the barbecue has eaten their fill of main course foods, there is hardly any room left for dessert. But for those who are confirmed dessert-lovers, a meal would not seem complete without something sweet to finish with. The recipes in this chapter offer the ideal solution.

The dishes that follow in the next few pages are light, yet full of flavor. There are three recipes to cook over the coals, a couple of fresh fruit salad combinations and an easy recipe for Giggle Cake that will keep the children happy. They will also love the Banana and Marshmallow Melts that are served oozing with butterscotch sauce, and there is even a recipe for addicted chocoholics – a fabulous Hot Chocolate Dip that is served with tropical fruit kebabs. Remember to keep some cream handy, and some ice cream in the freezer, just for those who can't resist the extra indulgence.

Make two or three of the recipes here if you are planning to make a real day of your barbecue party. And don't forget, people often wander back for more, even if they thought they were full up half an hour before. So make plenty, as all of these desserts are worth making room for!

Opposite: *Fresh fruits from home and abroad provide a delicious basis for some barbecued desserts.*

STEP 2

STEP 3

STEP 4

STEP 5

BANANA & MARSHMALLOW MELTS WITH BUTTERSCOTCH SAUCE

This simply delicious dessert will go down a treat with children of all ages. Bananas and marshmallows taste fantastic with the warm butterscotch sauce.

SERVES 4

4 wooden skewers
4 bananas
4 tbsp lemon juice
1 pkt marshmallows

SAUCE:
$1/2$ cup butter
$2/3$ cup light muscovado sugar
$1/3$ cup light corn syrup
4 tbsp hot water

1 Soak the wooden skewers in hand-hot water for 30 minutes.

2 Slice the bananas into large chunks, and dip them into the lemon juice to prevent them from going brown.

3 Thread the marshmallows and pieces of banana alternately onto kebab sticks or bamboo skewers, placing 3 marshmallows and 2 pieces of banana onto each one.

4 To make the sauce, melt the butter, sugar and syrup together in a small saucepan. Add the hot water, stirring until blended and smooth. Do not let it boil, or else the mixture will become toffee-like. Keep the sauce warm at the edge of the barbecue, stirring occasionally.

5 Sear the kebabs over the barbecue coals for 30–40 seconds, turning constantly, so that the marshmallows just begin to brown and melt.

6 Serve the kebabs with some of the butterscotch sauce spooned over.

TIPS

The warm butterscotch sauce tastes wonderful with vanilla ice cream. Make double the quantity of sauce if you plan to serve ice cream at the barbecue.

Ideally, prepare the kebabs just before they are cooked to prevent the bananas from turning brown. The sauce can be prepared ahead, though.

You can heat whole bananas in their skins over the barbecue. When blackened, split the skins and serve with a spoonful of the sauce.

STEP 1

STEP 2

STEP 3

STEP 4

CHAR-COOKED PINEAPPLE WITH GINGER & BROWN SUGAR BUTTER

Fresh pineapple slices are cooked on the barbecue, and brushed with a buttery fresh ginger and brown sugar baste.

SERVES 4

1 fresh pineapple

BUTTER:
¹/₂ cup butter
¹/₂ cup light muscovado sugar
1 tsp finely grated fresh gingerroot

TOPPING:
1 cup natural fromage frais
¹/₂ tsp ground cinnamon
1 tbsp light muscovado sugar

1 Prepare the fresh pineapple by cutting off the spiky top. Peel the pineapple with a sharp knife, and cut into thick slices.

2 To make the ginger-flavored butter, put the butter, sugar and gingerroot into a small saucepan, and heat slowly until melted. Transfer to a heatproof bowl, and keep warm at the side of the barbecue, ready for basting the fruit.

3 To prepare the topping, mix together the fromage frais, cinnamon and sugar. Cover and chill until ready to serve.

4 Barbecue the pineapple slices for about 2 minutes on each side, brushing them with the ginger butter baste.

5 Serve the pineapple with a little extra ginger butter sauce poured over. Top with a spoonful of the spiced fromage frais.

ALTERNATIVES

If you prefer, substitute ¹/₂ teaspoon ground ginger for the grated fresh gingerroot.

Light muscovado sugar gives the best flavor, but you can use ordinary soft brown sugar instead.

You can make this dessert indoors by cooking the pineapple under a hot broiler, basting it as above with the melted ginger butter.

STEP 2

STEP 3

STEP 3

STEP 4

TOASTED TROPICAL FRUIT KEBABS WITH HOT CHOCOLATE DIP

Spear some chunks of exotic tropical fruits onto kebab sticks, sear them over the barbecue, and serve with this amazing chocolate dip.

SERVES 4

4 wooden skewers

DIP:
4 squares dark chocolate, broken into pieces
2 tbsp light corn syrup
1 tbsp cocoa powder
1 tbsp cornstarch
generous ¾ cup milk

KEBABS:
1 mango
1 papaya
2 kiwi fruit
½ small pineapple
1 large banana
2 tbsp lemon juice
⅔ cup white rum

1 Soak the wooden skewers in hand-hot water for 30 minutes.

2 Put all the ingredients for the chocolate dip into a saucepan. Heat, stirring constantly, until thickened and smooth. Keep warm at the edge of the barbecue.

3 Slice the mango on each side of its large, flat pit. Cut the flesh into chunks, removing the peel. Halve, deseed and peel the papaya, and cut into chunks. Peel the kiwi fruit, and slice into chunks. Peel the pineapple, and cut into chunks. Peel and slice the banana, and dip the pieces in the lemon juice.

4 Thread the pieces of fruit alternately onto the wooden skewers. Place them in a shallow dish, and pour over the rum. Let them soak up the flavor of the rum until ready to barbecue, at least 30 minutes.

5 Cook the kebabs over the hot coals, turning frequently, until seared, about 2 minutes. Serve, accompanied by the hot chocolate dip.

VARIATIONS

Milk chocolate can be used in the chocolate dip instead of dark, and honey could be substituted for light corn syrup.

For the kebabs, use any fruit you like, providing it can be threaded onto skewers. Peaches, nectarines, apples and grapes are all suitable.

GIGGLE CAKE

It's a mystery how this cake got its name – perhaps it's because it's easy to make and fun to eat. It takes only minutes to put together.

STEP 1

SERVES 8

2 cups mixed dried fruit
1/2 cup butter or margarine
1 cup soft brown sugar
2 cups self-rising flour
pinch of salt
2 eggs, beaten
7 1/2-ounce can of chopped pineapple, drained
1/2 cup candied cherries, halved

1 Put the mixed dried fruit into a large bowl, and cover with boiling water. Let soak for 10–15 minutes, then drain well.

2 Put the butter or margarine and sugar into a large saucepan, and heat slowly until melted. Add the drained mixed dried fruit, and cook over a low heat, stirring frequently, for 4–5 minutes. Remove from the heat, and transfer to a mixing bowl. Let cool.

3 Sift the flour and salt into the dried fruit mixture, and stir well. Add the eggs, mixing until thoroughly incorporated.

4 Add the pineapples and cherries to the cake mixture, and stir to combine. Transfer the mixture to a greased and lined 2-pound loaf pan, and level the surface.

5 Bake in a preheated oven at 350°F for about 1 hour. Test the cake with a fine skewer; if it comes out clean, the cake is cooked. If not, return to the oven for a few more minutes.

STEP 2

STEP 3

VARIATIONS

If you wish, add 1 teaspoon ground apple pie spice to the cake mixture, sifting it in with the flour.

Bake the cake in a 7-in. round cake pan if you don't have a loaf pan of the right size. Remember to grease and line it first.

STEP 4

STEP 1

STEP 2

STEP 3

STEP 5

GREEN FRUIT SALAD WITH MINT & LEMON SYRUP

This delightful fresh fruit salad is the perfect finale for a summer barbecue. It has a lovely light syrup made with fresh mint and honey.

SERVES 4

1 small Charentais or honeydew melon
2 green apples
2 kiwi fruit
1 cup seedless green grapes
sprigs of fresh mint to decorate

SYRUP:
1 lemon
²/₃ cup white wine
²/₃ cup water
4 tbsp clear honey
few sprigs of fresh mint

1 To make the syrup, pare the rind from the lemon, using a potato peeler.

2 Put the lemon rind into a saucepan with the wine, water and honey. Heat and simmer slowly for 10 minutes. Remove from the heat. Add the sprigs of mint, and let cool.

3 Slice the melon in half, and scoop out the seeds. Use a melon baller or a teaspoon to make melon balls.

4 Core and chop the apples. Peel and slice the kiwi fruit.

5 Strain the cooled syrup into a serving bowl, removing and reserving the lemon rind, and discarding the mint sprigs. Add the apple, grapes, kiwi and melon. Stir through lightly to mix.

6 Serve, decorated with sprigs of fresh mint and some of the reserved lemon rind.

SERVING SUGGESTION

Serve the fruit salad in an attractive glass dish. Chill the dish for 20 minutes first, then keep the fruit salad cold by placing the dish in a large bowl of crushed ice or ice cubes.

STEP 1

STEP 2

STEP 3

STEP 4

BLACKBERRY, APPLE & FRESH FIG COMPOTE WITH HONEY YOGURT

Elderflower cordial is used in the syrup for this refreshing fruit compôte, giving it a delightfully summery flavor.

SERVES 4

1 lemon
¼ cup superfine sugar
4 tbsp elderflower cordial
1¼ cups water
4 eating apples
2 cups blackberries
2 fresh figs

TOPPING:
⅔ cup thick, creamy natural yogurt
2 tbsp clear honey

1 Pare the rind from the lemon, using a potato peeler. Squeeze the juice. Put the lemon rind and juice into a saucepan with the sugar, elderflower cordial and water. Heat slowly and simmer, uncovered, for 10 minutes.

2 Peel, core, and slice the apples, and add them to the saucepan. Simmer slowly for about 4–5 minutes until just tender. Let cool.

3 Transfer the apples and syrup to a serving bowl and add the blackberries. Slice and add the figs. Stir lightly to mix. Cover and chill until ready to serve.

4 Spoon the yogurt into a small serving bowl, and drizzle the honey over the top. Cover and chill, then serve with the fruit salad.

TIPS

Elderflower cordial is easy to obtain from supermarkets, health-food stores and delis. Alternatively, you can use a blackberry or apple cordial instead.

Do not prepare the apples until the syrup is ready, or they will begin to turn brown.

Fresh whipped cream is delicious served with this fruit salad. If you are choosing cream for whipping, buy either heavy cream or whipping cream. Heavy cream labeled as "extra thick" is suitable only for spooning, and will not whip.

USING A BARBECUE

TIPS FOR BARBECUING FOOD

First and foremost, treat food for barbecuing with care – it should be kept chilled in the refrigerator or in a cool box, complete with ice packs, until ready to cook.

Light the barbecue in plenty of time, remembering that you will need about 45 minutes for charcoal to heat and about 10–15 minutes for a gas barbecue to become hot enough.

Food cooks best over glowing embers, not smoking fuel, so avoid putting the food over the hot coals until the smoking has subsided.

Oil the barbecue rack lightly before adding the food, to help to prevent it from sticking, and oil the skewers, tongs, and barbecue fork for the same reason.

Control the heat by adjusting the distance of the food from the coals, or by altering the controls on a gas barbecue. Ideally, food should not be cooked too quickly, or else it will blacken and char on the outside before the middle is cooked – it needs time for the distinctive barbecued taste to be imparted.

VEGETABLES

For kebabs, choose a mixture of vegetables that will all cook at the same rate, and cut the chunks into roughly the same size. Choose from eggplants, tomatoes, sliced corn-on-the-cob or baby corn, mushrooms,

The recipes in *Vegetarian Barbecues* are a welcome alternative to all those summertime meat-eaters' feasts. This book offers simple, delicious barbecue dishes for people who are committed vegetarians, for those who cook for them, or just for anyone who enjoys eating tasty vegetarian food!

The very idea of vegetarian barbecues seems odd to many people, who would probably only be able to think of cooking vegetable kebabs or stuffed baked potatoes. Yet there are so many tasty and nutritious vegetarian recipes that can be cooked over hot coals – after all, barbecuing is just an alternative method of cooking by direct heat. Like broiling and roasting, barbecuing cooks food quickly, so it can be applied successfully to all sorts of vegetarian dishes, as this book shows.

There is certainly something special about food cooked outdoors – it always tastes so good! It is almost as if the fresh air itself permeates the food and contributes to its flavor. Or perhaps it is just that we enjoy the sunshine and relaxation that is all part of the barbecue scenario. Whatever the reason, there is no doubt that the aromas and flavors of barbecued food are truly wonderful. So make the most of the summer months by doing your cooking and entertaining outside. The recipes in this book have all been devised with speed, convenience and appetizing food in mind, so that cooking is less of a chore, and more like good fun!

CHOOSING YOUR BARBECUE

These days there are many different types of barbecue available, and your choice really depends on whether you think you will be going into barbecuing in a big way, or whether it will just be an occasional outdoor venture. The space available in your garden or on your patio will influence the size and type of equipment you choose – there's not much point in having a huge brick-built barbecue if your yard is the size of a postage stamp! Likewise, if you are only catering for small numbers, you may not need anything too grand.

Get a feel for what is available by having a good look around garden centers, supermarkets, cookware stores, department stores, and hardware stores. Before you buy, ask yourself a few questions about your needs – think about where you will use your barbecue and how often. Consider whether you want a portable type that can easily be lifted from one part of your garden to another. Will you be able to store the barbecue in winter and if so, does it dismantle easily? How big a barbecue do you need – are you cooking for crowds or just a cozy twosome? And is the barbecue the correct height? It could be very uncomfortable cooking on it if it is too low for you.

Whatever your constraints and considerations, it is always worth buying the best quality barbecue within your price range to give you good service. And for safety reasons, make sure that you uy one that is stable and sturdy, as it ould be very dangerous if not.

TYPES OF BARBECUE

Brick-built barbecues

or serious barbecuing, a brick-built onstruction is ideal, providing that you ave the room for a permanent fixture. Make sure that you position it wisely – ot too close to trees or the garden shed! The bricks do not have to be cemented ogether – if you prefer, they can be tacked so that the barbecue can be ismantled easily.

Self-assembly kits can be bought, vhich include a cooking grid, a charcoal rid, and a metal base. They usually also ontain pegs to be embedded into the vall of the barbecue to provide different evels for cooking the food. You will have o buy the bricks separately, which could e expensive, as you may need about a undred.

Wagon barbecues

These barbecues are usually quite large nd can be moved around on wheels – a ood idea if you want to position your arbecue near the house one day and in he evening sun the next, or move it from ne end of the patio to the other. They nay have hooks for hanging utensils and helves for barbecue equipment or for toring the charcoal.

The principle for barbecuing remains he same: the barbecue has a large ectangular area for the charcoal, above vhich is the grid to support the food. Check the storage possibilities for these ypes – some feature a removable fire

box, which enables the wagon to be folded flat. This is invaluable if you don't have a garage or shed in which to store your barbecue over the winter months, as a barbecue can be a cumbersome and messy thing to store.

Freestanding barbecues

These are a very popular choice for people with small gardens and patios, and for those who just use them occasionally. They are supported on legs, bringing them to a sensible working height.

Freestanding barbecues can be round or rectangular, and they vary in their degree of sophistication – some have variable heights for the cooking grid, shelves, a wind shield, a warming rack or serving shelf, and a rod for spit-roasting food. Choose the right size, shape, and quality for your needs at a price that is within your budget.

Portable barbecues

These are particularly suitable for cooking food for a small number of people, and are ideal for setting onto a firm base or tabletop to work from. It is usually possible to move the food closer to the heat by means of notches set at varying heights above the coals into which the grid can be slotted. Fold-up versions are often available.

Disposable barbecues

Ideal for picnics, beach barbecues, or camping, these are designed to be used only once. Small and cheap to buy, they consist of a foil tray with specially impregnated coals. A grid supports the

and zucchini. New potatoes, onions, carrots, parsnips, and Jerusalem artichokes can also be barbecued, but will need a little precooking first.

If you are going to serve baked potatoes, cook them first too – either conventionally or in a microwave oven for speed. Wrap in foil, and keep warm to one side of the barbecue, ready for filling with one of the delicious ideas suggested on page 22. Alternatively, you can finish cooking potatoes directly on the grid over the coals, barbecuing them until the skins are crisp and brown.

Vegetables can be cooked in foil packages as well as on kebab skewers. Slice them roughly, sprinkle with olive oil, herbs, and seasonings, and wrap tightly. Cook over the barbecue until tender – test with a skewer to check whether they are done.

HERBS

Have some fresh herbs to hand for throwing onto the coals. They smell wonderful as they burn and will add extra flavor to your food. Woody herbs, such as rosemary, thyme, and bay leaves, burn slowly, so they are good choices.

SALADS AND SIDE DISHES
Keep salads and other accompaniments fresh and chilled in the refrigerator, or in a cool box with ice packs. Ask for some help in carrying them outside when the barbecued food is almost cooked. Have plates, flatware, and serving spoons at the ready, so that there is no need to keep dashing indoors. And don't forget the salt and pepper!

DESSERTS
It is a good idea to serve a selection of desserts at barbecues – nothing too fancy or complicated is needed, just something to refresh the palate or provide a change of taste. Fresh fruit salads are always a good choice, and a couple of different types of fruit kebab will go down well, particularly if served with a delicious sauce. See the Desserts chapter for some mouthwatering suggestions.

COOKING TIME
Cooking times for barbecuing are difficult to give exactly, as it will depend on how fierce the heat is, the distance of the food from the coals, and the type of food being cooked. Test the food from time to time to check whether it is done to your liking.

food as it cooks, and there is sufficient fuel to last for about an hour.

Gas barbecues
Charcoal is abandoned in this type of barbecue, and gas is used to heat lava rocks instead. These models are quick and convenient to use, as you don't have to light the coals and wait the same length of time before the barbecue is ready. The special rocks heat through in about 15 minutes.

Another advantage of lava rocks is that they can be used over and over again, although they will need replacing occasionally – you will know when to do this, as the rocks will begin to flare up frequently during cooking. The food cooks in the same way over the "coals," and achieves the same delicious taste, as the hot oil or liquid from the food drips down onto the rocks and creates the smoke that gives the food its distinctive barbecued flavor.

Portable gas barbecues and larger, more sophisticated wagon-types often have adjustable heat settings. These are especially suitable for bigger events, and for families who hold barbecues regularly, as they are ready quickly, and can be kept burning for a long time more easily than charcoal barbecues.

BARBECUE FUEL
Charcoal is used to fuel most barbecues, with the exception of gas-fired types, which heat lava rocks instead. Charcoal is available as briquettes, which burn the longest, or lumpwood, which is easier to ignite. It is also possible to buy "barbecue fuel," which is a charcoal substitute,

although you may find that this does not burn quite so well.

Always remember to store charcoal and barbecue fuel in a dry place – if it is allowed to get damp, it may take you a long time to ignite it.

SAFETY TIPS
Choose a safe place for setting up your barbecue. It must be on a level surface, away from trees, bushes, fences, and sheds. Try to position the barbecue well away from children's play areas, and avoid setting it up in a place where your guests would hamper your activities.

Take great care when lighting a barbecue – and *never* use gasoline, paraffin, or methylated spirits. You can buy special gels and liquids for lighting barbecues, but always read the instructions on the package first. You may need some extra-long matches or tapers to help you to ignite the barbecue.

Keep children well away from the barbecue – they don't always realize how hot it is. If they want to help, offer them a job threading food onto kebab skewers (if they are old enough to cope with this safely), or bringing things out from the kitchen.

Have a bucket of sand ready to throw over the barbecue in case there are any mishaps and it catches fire – soil makes a good alternative. Neither improve the taste of the food, so take care that it doesn't happen!

ACCESSORIES
Make sure that you are well-equipped with utensils that will make the cook's life easier when standing at the barbecue

set of long tongs, a barbecue fork, plenty of long skewers, and a pancake turner for serving the food will all come in handy. Long-handled brushes for basting the food with marinades and sauces will also be required. A couple of old saucepans are very useful for heating sauces and keeping them warm on the metal grid.

Some barbecues have rôtisserie attachments, which are ideal for cooking large pieces of meat. These are only suitable if you have plenty of room on your barbecue, but are excellent for ensuring the meat is evenly cooked.

For safety, have a thick pair of potholders at the ready for picking up hot skewers or hot handles. Protect your clothes too, and wear a great big apron! Plastic aprons are good, as they wipe clean easily.

PLANNING YOUR BARBECUE

Timing
Make your life easier by preparing lots of tasty food that doesn't take forever to cook – check the ideas in this book for inspiration. Whenever food is being barbecued, there always seems to be a long wait – even though it may only be minutes – so have a few dips and nibbles for your hungry guests. These can all be made ahead and kept chilled until needed. Raw vegetable crudités can be chopped and prepared beforehand too – just keep them chilled in sealed plastic bags until ready to serve.

Barbecues always take longer to get going than you expect, so allow plenty of time. Don't be tempted to start cooking too soon, or the coals will not be ready. The flames should have died down and the coals reduced to a steady glow before you begin.

Don't attempt to cook for a large party on a small barbecue, as it could take hours to feed everyone! In this situation, it is better to cook most of the food in the kitchen, and provide only a few barbecued items. Vegetarian sausages and burgers are ideal, as they cook quickly and can be barbecued in large quantities even on a small barbecue.

Planning ahead
Many foods for barbecuing will benefit from being marinated, especially dishes using tofu or TVP, which will absorb the flavor of the marinade – the longer they can be left to soak up the flavors, the better they will taste. You can buy tofu in four varieties – smoked, firm, soft, or silken; use smoked or firm for kebabs, soft for adding to burgers, and silken for adding to sauces and dips.

Have your kebabs ready-threaded for quick cooking; if possible, choose flat metal skewers so that the food does not slide as the kebabs are turned. Alternatively, use bamboo sticks – but remember to soak these in water beforehand so that they do not burn over the hot coals.

Make both sweet and savoury sauces in advance if you can – for example, the Tasty Barbecue sauce, the butterscotch sauce for the Banana and Marshmallow Melts, and the Hot Chocolate Dip for the Tropical Fruit Kebabs can all be prepared ahead of time, leaving you with plenty of time to relax and enjoy your barbecue.

CLEANING UP!
When you have enjoyed the barbecue and all the food is finished, you only have the clearing up left to do! The best idea is to delegate – after all, you've already done the preparation, so let someone else do the cleaning jobs.

Your barbecue equipment will appreciate being looked after, and it will last longer too, so do take care of it. Before attempting to clean it, let the embers become completely cold.

Empty the ashes and use a wire brush to clean the barbecue rack. If necessary, use one of the proprietary barbecue cleaning products to remove any stubborn stains.

Pack the barbecue away if it is portable, or dismantle it and store it in a dry place at the end of the season, ready for its reappearance next summer.

It is always worth buying fresh charcoal or fuel after a barbecue, to be sure of having enough the next time. This way an impromptu barbecue is not spoiled by not being able to get hold of a bag of charcoal at just the right moment. Store the fuel in a warm, dry place away from any heat source or naked flames. Keep well out of the reach of children, and make sure also that lighter fluids and cleaning fluids are securely capped and stored out of reach.

INDEX